Communication
and
Conflict
Resolution

A Biblical Perspective

Stuart Scott

ISBN 1 885904-50-9

Printed in the United States of America

Published by FOCUS PUBLISHING, INC.

CONTENTS

GOOD COMMUNICATION

One of the biggest obstacles to a good marriage is poor communication. We could even say that a marriage relationship is only as good as a couple's ability to send and receive the right message. We will see from Scripture that good communication from God's perspective is sending a message that is **holy, purposeful, clear** and **timely**.

Communication is the vehicle that is used to accomplish many responsibilities and relational aspects of marriage. One can neither address issues without it, nor resolve conflict without it. How we communicate with one another will produce either good or bad consequences. If we communicate poorly, it will have a negative effect on the marriage relationship. (Some of the following is adapted from *Strengthening your Marriage*, by Wayne Mack.)[1]

Some negative effects of poor communication are:

- God will not be honored by a good testimony for Christ.
- The relationship will be superficial and strained.
- Discord and conflict will be common.
- Issues will remain unclear and unresolved.
- Wrong ideas will remain uncorrected.
- Bitterness will begin to set in.
- Wise decision-making will be thwarted.
- The temptation will be great to communicate with another person outside the marriage.

On the other hand, if we communicate in a God-honoring way, it will have a very positive impact on the marriage relationship.

Some positive effects of good communication are:

- God is honored by a good testimony for Christ.
- The relationship will be strengthened and be meaningful.

- Companionship and oneness will be enjoyed more.
- Harmony will be present.
- Any disagreement can be handled quickly and without conflict.
- Problem issues can be clarified and resolved.
- Wrong ideas can be corrected.
- Forgiveness and trust will be exercised easier.
- Good decision-making will be enhanced.

Good Communication Is Important to God

Even more important than the fact that good communication is crucial to the marriage relationship is the fact that good communication is extremely important to God. It involves self-control and discipline—character qualities that the Christian must possess. Communication involves ruling our spirit, our tongue, and our body, and going against our feelings when they contradict what we know to be true. Communication involves the heart, which is of the greatest importance to God. He often addresses our communication to expose the heart, because our communication is ruled by what is in our heart. Jesus said:

> **You brood of vipers, how can you, being evil, speak what is good? For the mouth speaks out of that which fills the heart.**
> **Matthew 12:34**

This area of the Christian life is so important to God that the Bible is full of commands and principles on communication. (See especially Ephesians 4:25, 29, 31-32; Psalm 141:3, Proverbs 21:23, 25:11, and Proverbs 18:13,17).

Perhaps the most crucial element of communication is our speech. It is certainly the most obvious. The Word of God teaches us that if a person can control his tongue he will be a godly man and able to control all of his passions.

> **For we all stumble in many ways. If anyone does not stumble in what he says, he is a perfect man, able to bridle the whole body as well.**
> **James 3:2**

Being in control of what we say and how we say it is a great virtue in God's sight, and can bring Him great glory. Not being careful about our communication, however, can do a great deal of damage and therefore dishonor God.

> **See how great a forest is set aflame by such a small fire! And the tongue is a fire, the very world of iniquity; the tongue is set among our members as that which defiles the entire body, and sets on fire the course of our life, and is set on fire by hell.**
> **James 3:5b-6**

Persons who communicate in a way that displeases God should not think that they are godly men and women. You may be a deacon or a Sunday school teacher in your church, but your communication will reveal the kind of person you really are, because what comes out of your mouth is usually what is in your heart. If you truly desire to exemplify Christ you will seek to become a good communicator. Everything that Jesus Christ communicated was **holy, clear, purposeful, and timely**. With a prayer for God's help, let's seek to understand the prerequisites and the mechanics of this kind of communication.

Six Prerequisites to Good Communication

1. *You must want to please God more than anything else.* You must want to please God more than to have your own way. You must want to please God more than to be right. You must want to please God more than to be vindicated.

   > **Therefore we also have as our ambition, whether at home or absent, to be pleasing to Him.**
   > **2 Corinthians 5:9**

2. *You must be humble.* It takes a great deal of humility to communicate for the right reasons, and to not react in pride to something that is being said by the other person. A humble man is a patient man. If you are humble you will be patient when what you say is misunderstood, or when you don't like what another is trying to say to you.

> **Therefore I, the prisoner of the Lord, implore you to walk in a manner worthy of the calling with which you have been called, with all humility and gentleness, with patience, showing tolerance for one another in love, being diligent to preserve the unity of the Spirit in the bond of peace.**
> **Ephesians 4:1-3**

3. *You must be aware that you are accountable to God for everything you communicate.* God hears our every word and will hold us accountable for them.

> **But I tell you that every careless word that people speak, they shall give an accounting for it in the day of judgment.**
> **Matthew 12:36**

4. *You must know how to listen.* Good communication is dependent on good listening skills. James says, "everyone must be quick to hear, slow to speak and slow to become angry" (1:19). James means that we need to listen more than we speak. Unfortunately many of us do just the opposite, especially in the midst of a disagreement. Some of us will not let the other person get a word in edgewise. This talkativeness could be because we believe that only we could have anything valuable to say, because we simply like to hear ourselves talk, or because we are desperately trying to get our own way or be proven right.

If a person is not a good listener, he will most likely jump to conclusions. If he jumps to conclusions he will most likely say or do the wrong thing. We are warned about speaking before we have really heard what others have to say:

> **He who gives an answer before he hears, it is folly and shame to him.**
> **Proverbs 18:13**

Listening well means:

• Concentrating on and carefully considering what the other person is saying.

- Not interrupting (some rare exceptions may apply, e. g., someone who never stops talking, or when someone is out of control).
- Not formulating what you are going to say while the other person is talking.
- Not talking too much, but allowing breaks in the conversation so that another person can have time to process information, formulate what they want to say and then say it to you.
- When you are in an important conversation, always ask for clarification with comments like, "Could you say that again?" or "Could you explain a little more?" or "Is this what you are saying...?"
- Not talking when someone else is speaking. This bad manner is a serious offense.

5. *You must know that communication involves more than just words.* Communication involves words, tone of voice, body language, and deeds. It is a well-known fact that the words we speak are only one avenue of our communication. We can say two completely different things by changing our tone of voice and body language. Take the phrase, "Could you please come here?" Put on an angry face, shake your index finger, and put a great deal of emphasis on the word please and you have a harsh comment. Say the same words, however, with a smile and a warm, coaxing tone of voice, and you have communicated a very different message. We can even cancel out our words if everything else about us says the opposite.

You must be very careful about:

- The volume of your voice
- The tone of your voice
- Facial expressions
- Hand gestures
- Sighing, or in some cases, snorting
- Rolling the eyes
- A look of amazement or disgust
- Body posture

Ask your spouse to help you recognize any wrong use of these very counter-productive means of communication.

Communication also involves deeds. Sometimes our actions speak louder than our words. Sometimes they speak differently than our words. If we say to our wives "I want to spend time with you today," and then tinker around in the garage or in the yard all day, what are we really communicating? Be sure that your deeds communicate the same thing as your words. Don't just say what is right, do what is right.

> **Therefore, to one who knows the right thing to do and does not do it, to him it is sin.**
> **James 4:17**

6. *You must be willing to put forth the effort and spend the time it takes to communicate.* A husband who is self-serving will most likely not communicate well. Likewise wives who show little interest in their husband's concerns. We need to talk when we don't want to talk and listen when we don't want to listen. Many husbands find it difficult to talk and listen after a hard day's work, especially if their job is people-oriented. This, however, is where the husband must die to self.

Some husbands may not be gifted in speaking to groups of people, but they must speak to their wives and families in order to love and shepherd them. The less we speak, the harder it will before others to avoid assuming what is going on inside of us. Just because we are ill, tired, or not much of a talker, we are not released from the responsibility to work at good communication.

> **Be devoted to one another in brotherly love; give preference to one another in honor; not lagging behind in diligence, fervent in spirit, serving the Lord; rejoicing in hope, persevering in tribulation, devoted to prayer.**
> **Romans 12:10-12**

Biblical Principles of Verbal Communication

Two General Principles

A great deal of our communication involves our speech. We are continually using words to communicate with others. It is very important that we know what God has to say about speech in particular. King David and his son, King Solomon, give us two general principles to remember.

1. We must truly desire to guard our lips. We must put great importance on honoring God with our speech. David prayed:

> **Set a guard, O Lord, over my mouth; keep watch over the door of my lips.**
> **Psalm 141:3**

2. We must understand that if we <u>do</u> guard our lips, we will avoid all kinds of trouble. King Solomon, who also told us to "guard our heart" (Proverbs 4:23), said:

> **He who guards his mouth and his tongue, guards his soul from troubles.**
> **Proverbs 21:23**

With these general principles in mind, we can get more specific about our speech. We are going to relate four principles to the qualities of Christ's communication mentioned earlier. His communication was: **holy, purposeful, clear, and timely.**

Four Specific Principles

1. Christ's communication was **Holy**: (truthful and righteous)
What you say must be *the truth.*

> **Therefore, laying aside falsehood, speak truth each one of you with his neighbor, for we are members of one another.**
> **Ephesians 4:25**

Everything Christ said was completely true. As believers who want to exemplify Him, we must be sure that we are totally honest. This statement means there will be no form of deceit in what we say, and that everything we say will agree with God's truth. We will be very careful that what we say is accurate. God hates lying.

> There are six things which the Lord hates, yes, seven
> which are an abomination to Him: .... a lying tongue ....
> **Proverbs 6:16-17a**

There are many forms of deceit we must guard against.

- An outright lie
  This would be a complete fabrication or contradiction of the truth
  (e.g., Satan, Genesis 3:4).
- An exaggeration—going further than the truth
  The truth plus a lie always equals a lie (e.g., Esau, Genesis 25:32).
- A half or partial truth— giving only part of the information, so as
  to lead a person to believe something that is not really true or to
  cover up the truth (e.g., Abraham, Genesis 12:13)
- An evasion of the truth—changing the subject, not really
  answering the question, causing another problem to divert
  attention (e.g., Cain, Genesis 4:9).

How you say it must be righteous.

> Let no unwholesome word proceed from your
> mouth.... Do not grieve the Holy Spirit of God, by
> whom you were sealed for the day of redemption. Let
> all bitterness and wrath and anger and clamor and
> slander be put away from you, along with all malice.
> Be kind to one another, tender-hearted, forgiving each
> other, just as God in Christ also has forgiven you.
> **Ephesians 4:29-32**

This principle is why we must rule our spirit and our words, no
matter what the other person does. Christ was always in control and
holy in how He communicated. You will not be able to control what
others say, but by God's grace you can control how you respond.

Our speech must be without:

- Bitterness: a fixed attitude of sharpness or harshness
- Wrath: a temporary outburst of anger

- Anger: a slow burn of indignation
- Clamor: yelling, loud quarreling, harsh contention
- Slander: speaking evil of a person, like name-calling, belittling, attacking the person, etc.
- Malice: speech designed to injure or make someone suffer

Instead, our speech must be with:

- Kindness: gracious, easy, courteous, good, helpful
- Tenderheartedness: compassionate, sympathetic
- Forgiveness: giving up on revenge or a grudge

> **He who is slow to anger is better than the mighty, and**
> **he who rules his spirit, than he who captures a city.**
> **Proverbs 16:32**

You must be careful not to enter into sin even if your spouse is sinning. Answer in a godly way and a way that convicts them of their own foolishness. This guideline also applies to answering an angry person or a manipulative person.

> **Do not answer a fool** *according to his folly*, **or you**
> **will also be like him. Answer a fool** *as his folly*
> *deserves*, **that he not be wise in his own eyes.**
> **Proverbs 26:4-5 [emphasis mine]**

Remember, our actions (in this case our words) are directly connected to our thoughts. If you are going to be successful in practicing right responses, you must begin at the level of your thoughts. Seek to isolate the thoughts that lead to the wrong ways of speaking.

2. Christ's communication was **Purposeful**: Your motivation for what you say must be *unselfish*.

For God's glory: "**...Do all to the glory of God.**" **1 Corinthians 10:31b**

For others' good: "**...Only such a word as is good for edification**
according to the need of the moment, so that it will
give grace to those who hear." **Ephesians 4:29**

Christ's purposes were God the Father's purposes, and they were always unselfish. If we are not careful we can communicate for the wrong reasons. We should not speak in order to get our selfish or fleshly desires met or to retaliate. Until we are confident that our purpose in speaking is for God's glory and for the other's good, we would do better to remain quiet. Pray for the right motive.

If our motives are right, we will:

*   Act, not react according to feelings or pride
*   Attack the problem, not the person
*   Say only what will accomplish good
*   Be solution-oriented

We need to be aware that this is another area where "the flesh wars against the spirit." Expect your flesh to rear its ugly head but be ready, by God's grace, to deny it and control it. If we want our speech to accomplish good purposes, we will always be gracious in how we speak and we will not use any wrong methods of speech. This idea is explained by Paul in Colossians:

> **Let your speech always be with grace, as though seasoned with salt, so that you will know how you should respond to each person.**
> **Colossians 4:6**

Having gracious speech is likened to something that is seasoned with salt. Salt makes food palatable or tasty and preserves it from corruption. We need to make our words as palatable as possible and as preserving as possible.

Also, our words will not be able to accomplish good purposes if we do not have all the information. Be sure that you have *all* the facts and information and *accurate* facts and information. Ask questions (Proverbs 18:13).

3. Christ's communication was **Clear**: *The way* you say it must be *straight-forward and appropriate.*

> **But let your statement be, 'Yes, yes' or 'No, no'; anything beyond these is of evil.**
> **Matthew 5:37**

Christ was a master at getting to the heart of the matter when He communicated. Every word He spoke was perfectly suited to the situation. There were times when He spoke in parables for the express purpose of not being understood by those who really weren't interested in following Him or because the time was not right (Matthew 13:10-16). But this approach was taken for God's purposes and is not normally how He spoke to the disciples. Christ was a man of few words. He never said more than what needed to be said. Many words can make a message unclear and also lead to sin.

> **When there are many words, transgression is unavoidable, but he who restrains his lips is wise.**
> **Proverbs 10:19**

The passages above teach clearly that we need to be straightforward (but loving) in our speech, and as brief and appropriate as possible. We need to learn how to get to the heart of the matter wisely, and fittingly. It is impossible to be straightforward, brief, and appropriate, unless we think carefully about what we are going to say.

> **The heart of the righteous *ponders how to answer*, but the mouth of the wicked pours out evil things.**
> **Proverbs 15:28 [emphasis mine]**

If we are going to be clear we will:

- Pray about what to say.
- Think carefully about what needs to be said.
- Speak concisely.
- Refrain from withholding information or frustrating people by saying things like, "I'm not going to tell you. You should know!"
- Discuss mutual definitions. For example, someone might tell you "When you say 'That's different,' what I incorrectly understand is, 'That's stupid,' so don't say that anymore."
- Use no manipulative tactics. Say what you mean. Don't hint or say something to make others feel guilty so they will do what you want.

4. Christ's communication was **Timely**: *When* you say it the time needs to be *right*.

Like apples of gold in settings of silver is a word spoken in right circumstances
Proverbs 25:11

Christ always communicated at the perfect time. There are two principles concerning when we should communicate. We must communicate *as soon as time and situation will allow* and at *a good time*. We must not put off saying what needs to be said or dealing with a conflict any longer than is necessary. When we wait without good reason, we are giving the devil an opportunity to use the situation for evil.

Choosing the right time to speak will help good communication to take place. It is not being wise to deal with something important when there is really not enough time, when we or the other person are extremely tired, or when we know that the other person is either not in a very good frame of mind or distracted. A wise person will carefully choose his time to communicate.

To be timely we need to:

- Communicate something that needs to be communicated as soon as it is prudent. Don't wait needlessly.
- Have adequate time to communicate what needs to be communicated and give the other person a chance to respond.
- Be sure that the time you choose is the best time for all those involved.

Are You Truly Resolved?

Believers must be fully resolved to pursue godly communication. It is not easy to create new habits, but with God's help you can continue to improve at communicating His way. Unless you truly desire to honor God in this aspect of your marriage, the relationship will never be what it could be. Communicating in a God-honoring way involves having the right heart (one that is humble and wants to please God), some good listening skills and a willingness to die to self. Then, we must work to make our communication **holy, clear, purposeful, and timely**.

[1] Wayne Mack, *Strengthening Your Marriage*, Phillipsburg, NJ: Presbyterian and Reformed Publishing Co., 1977), p. 60.

CONFLICT RESOLUTION

It has been said, "Marriage is made in heaven, but so are thunder and lightning." Many marriages are characterized by conflict. For God's people, this should not be so. Any Christian couple can learn to dwell together in unity. I am not saying that Christian couples will always see *everything* eye to eye or even *never* offend one another. What I am saying is that true Christians can learn how to keep from fighting with one another. Even just one partner can keep a conflict from happening (Proverbs 15:18). Every Christian can and must know how to biblically avoid and resolve conflicts with their spouse.

Exactly What is a Conflict?

When we talk about conflict we are not talking about having a difference of opinion with someone or disagreeing with someone. We are not even talking about being offended or offending someone. These things can happen without conflict. The Latin word from which we get the word *conflict* means *to strike*. Conflict is a common military term which means to *fight against*. When two people have a conflict they may have a physical fight and/or a verbal fight, but both people are involved and against one another. Conflict, then, is *when both parties sin against one another (in their communication and/or their actions) and are then in opposition to one another.*

What Does God Think of Conflict?

Conflict is a grievous thing to God. He wants His children to have no part in it. The Bible is full of commands about controlling our words and our spirit, full of warnings about strife, and full of instruction on what to do if someone is angry with us or sinning against us. God wants His children to pursue peace:

13

**Walk in a manner worthy of the calling with which
you have been called, ... being diligent to preserve
the unity of the Spirit in the bond of peace.**
Ephesians 4:1,3

Most conflicts begin with some sort of offense. God wants us to do
everything we can to not offend anyone. Sometimes a person will take
offense at the Word of God or even the truth spoken in love. We cannot always avoid offending someone when we love them enough to tell
them what they need to hear. What God does *not* want us to do is needlessly or sinfully offend someone. This offense does not bring Him
glory. Not offending others is the context of the following verse.

**Whether, then, you eat or drink or whatever you do,
do all to the glory of God. Give no offense either to
Jews or to Greeks or to the church of God.**
1 Corinthians 10:31-32

Not only are we to be careful that we do not offend others, but God
tells us to love, pray for, and do good to those who sin against us. We
are to return good even to our enemies (Romans 12:21). Taking part in
conflict is never an option to God. When we choose to sin in this way
we are not acting like His children at all.

**But I say to you, love your enemies and pray for those
who persecute you, so that you may be sons of your
Father who is in heaven; for He causes His sun to rise
on the evil and the good, and sends rain on the righteous and the unrighteous.**
Matthew 5:44-45

We have already seen what God thinks of the thoughts, words, and
actions that are involved in sinful communication. Sinful communication is always involved in conflict. When Christ was addressing His
disciples in Matthew 5, He said:

**You have heard that the ancients were told, "You shall
not commit murder" and "Whoever commits murder
shall be liable to the court." But I say to you that
everyone who is angry with his brother shall be guilty**

**before the court; and whoever says to his brother,
"You good for nothing [empty head]," shall be guilty
before the supreme court; and whoever says, "You
fool [wicked-hearted person]," shall be guilty enough
to go into the fiery hell.**
Matthew 5:21-22 [explanation mine]

Here, Jesus puts being angry with someone on the same level as murder. He goes on to show that expressing that anger is even worse! Conflict is a serious thing to God. Christians should work to rid their marriage of it.

Where Do Conflicts Come From?

Differences

Conflicts can arise out of personal differences and differences of opinion. People are very different from one another. They have different abilities, different amounts of knowledge, different likes and dislikes, and different perspectives. This is something we need to accept as the norm. It is true that the more a couple has in common, the more they will see things in the same way. This does not mean that couples have to have a great deal in common in order to get along. Nor does it mean that they will necessarily have less conflict if they have a great deal in common. A couple can have a great deal in common and still have conflict if they are proud and selfish. Some say there is no hope for couples who are not compatible. This is obviously not God's perspective because when the Bible was written, many couples who married hardly knew each other, if at all (Genesis 24:1-4).

Having little in common does mean, however, that you must work to know one another well, appreciate one another, and see things from one another's perspective. These attitudes are certainly possible to attain, and working on them is a tremendous exercise in real love (Ephesians 4:2-3). I remember one couple in particular who came to see me. They were as different as two people could be and were very disturbed about the frequent conflicts in their marriage. They were a young Christian couple, active in ministry who sincerely loved the

Lord. Because of their commitment to their marriage and to the Lord, they began working hard at knowing, appreciating, and trying to understand things from the other's perspective. They now consider this one of the most rewarding times of their lives and are the dearest people in the world to one another. The more you work at knowing, appreciating, and understanding the perspective of your spouse, the more you will love her. Husband, *you* must take the lead in this endeavor if there are significant differences between you and your wife. Be encouraged! Spouses who are very different *can* experience companionship and oneness.

One of the things that can help very differing spouses the most is growth in God's Word. The more we have God's Word in common as husbands and wives, the more we will agree. The more each mind is renewed (changed) by Scripture, the more similarly a couple will think (Romans 12:2). One of the worst things a couple can do is work to change one another into each other's likeness. They are to be changed, rather, into Christ's likeness. The more a couple works at love and becoming one, the more differences will be accepted and blended to enhance the marriage.

Offenses

A very serious cause of conflict is a wrong response to an offense or to a sinning spouse. There is no reason an offense or someone else's sin must lead to a conflict in which both parties are sinning. Husbands and wives need to learn how to respond humbly and graciously to one another's sin and how to follow God's instructions for speaking the truth in love (Proverbs 27:6). We must control our responses to fit God's rules of communication and the proper handling of sin.

> **He who restrains his words has knowledge, and he
> who has a cool spirit is a man of understanding.**
> **Proverbs 17:27**

Pride and the Flesh

Whether a conflict arises out of a difference or an offense, it always involves sin. It ultimately stems from self-exalting pride, self-serving lusts, or both. The Proverbs tell us, "an arrogant man stirs up strife" (Proverbs 28:25) and "by pride comes nothing but strife" (Proverbs 13:10; NKJV). We have already addressed pride and humility a great deal (see booklet, "From Pride to Humility"), but it is important that we grasp the connection between pride and conflict. Husbands and wives must be humble if they wish to live in harmony.

Our fleshly lusts are another basic cause of conflict. James rebukes his readers in this way:

> **What is the source of quarrels and conflicts among you? Is not the source your pleasures that wage war in your members?** *You lust and do not have;* **so you commit murder. You are** *envious and cannot obtain;* **so you fight and quarrel. You do not have because you do not ask. You ask and do not receive, because you ask with wrong motives,** *so that you may spend it on your pleasures.*
> **James 4:1-3 [emphasis mine]**

James is telling us that the quarrels and conflicts in which we find ourselves are the outworking or the "deeds" of our fleshly lusts. Paul puts it another way:

> **Now the deeds of the flesh are evident, which are: immorality, impurity, sensuality, idolatry, sorcery,** *enmities, strife, jealousy, outbursts of anger, disputes, dissensions, factions, envying,* **drunkenness, carousing, and things like these, of which I forewarn you, just as I have forewarned you, that those who practice such things will not inherit the kingdom of God.**
> **Galatians 5:19-21 [emphasis mine]**

James' terminology is perfect for understanding the root cause of many conflicts. Several of the Greek words that James uses are military terms, like our term *conflict*. In many contexts, the word for "quarrels" means *military campaigns or chronic states of war*. The word for "conflicts" means *separate conflicts within a war*, or *small battles*. With these words James is conveying the idea of our being in opposition to one

Encamped Lusts

GOD

1 Peter 5:5 God is opposed to the PROUD

Quarrels and Conflicts

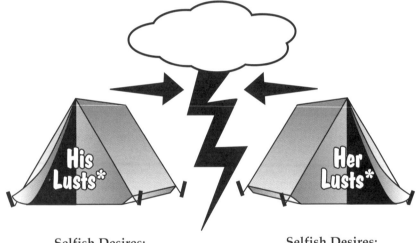

His Lusts*

Her Lusts*

Selfish Desires:
My Way
My Feelings
My Rights
My Expectations
My Needs
My Plans

Selfish Desires:
My Way
My Feelings
My Rights
My Expectations
My Needs
My Plans

PROUD and Fleshly

PROUD and Fleshly

*Lusts = Evil Desires and/or good desires turned lustful

another. He goes on to explain exactly what causes this opposition. It comes from the things we intently long for ("lust") or hotly desire ("envy"), but cannot obtain. Conflicts happen when we *must* have something. Our desires may even be good desires in and of themselves, but when they become demands, they are sinful. It is as if we set up a military encampment to obtain whatever it is we want so badly. If we picture our desires as military tents, the tent pegs become firmly planted and the battle begins.

When our goal becomes fulfilling our fleshly desires, we *will* have conflict. If Christian's are going to successfully stop participating in battle, they must be able to recognize fleshly lusts.

Some things that are fleshly lusts if pursued for self-gratification are:

- Riches
- Sex
- Food
- Possessions
- Relaxation/comfort
- Enjoyable or extreme experiences
- Recognition/approval

In the midst of a conflict ask yourself, "What is it I am wanting for myself?" If we are to stay out of or resolve conflict, our focus must be the good of others instead of self.

Let no one seek his own good, but that of his neighbor.
1 Corinthians 10:24

A man or woman who is engaged in conflict is focused on self and not on loving his or her spouse and glorifying God. Paul tells us that love "does not seek it's own, is not provoked" and "does not take into account a wrong suffered" (1 Corinthians 13:5)." When we are humble and loving, we will not seek to please self and we will not engage in conflict.

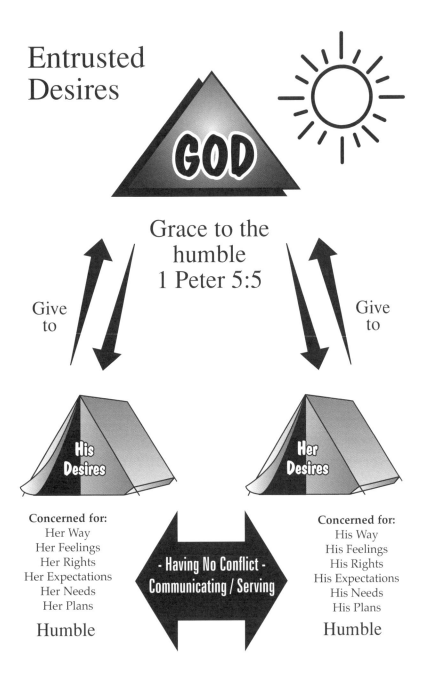

Entrusted
Desires

GOD

Grace to the
humble
1 Peter 5:5

Give
to

Give
to

His
Desires

Her
Desires

Concerned for:
Her Way
Her Feelings
Her Rights
Her Expectations
Her Needs
Her Plans

Humble

- Having No Conflict -
Communicating / Serving

Concerned for:
His Way
His Feelings
His Rights
His Expectations
His Needs
His Plans

Humble

We know that sin begins in one's mind. Our proud and fleshly thoughts can be likened to the seeds of conflict. We must do away with these sinful seeds before they spring up and cause conflict. We must replace proud or fleshly thinking if we hope to avoid conflict. Here are some thoughts that can cause conflict, and replacements for them:

Thoughts that lead to conflict:	Thoughts that avoid conflict:
That's ridiculous! I *will* have my way! How dare she! I will not be treated this way!	She may have a point. I don't have to have my way. I need to pray for him. How can I return good to her?

Can Differences and Disagreements Be Beneficial?

Yes! Differences and disagreements *can* be beneficial. We have already seen that they can be a beginning point to the development of real love, when we purpose to appreciate our spouse despite our differences. Here are some other benefits of differences and disagreements:

- They can encourage us to search the Scriptures (Psalm 119:71-72).
- They can help us think carefully about how and what we think or what we believe (Proverbs 15:28).
- They can help us work harder at communicating effectively (Ephesians 4:25).
- They can produce maturity and endurance (James 1:2-5).
- They can help us sharpen one another (Proverbs 27:17).
- They can strengthen our faith in the truth that God is working all things together for good (Romans 8:28-29).
- They give us opportunity to practice servanthood and preferring one another (Philippians 2:2-3).
- They give us opportunity to love and glorify God (1 Corinthians 10:31-32).

How Do We Avoid Conflicts?

We have seen that there are three sure-fire ways to *start* a conflict: wrong thoughts, wrong words, and/or wrong actions. A good question is, "How can we *avoid* one?" This is an important question to ask because there are wrong and right ways to avoid a conflict.

Some sinful ways to avoid conflict:

- *Just keep quiet*. Many married couples choose to avoid conflict in ways that are not acceptable to God. While there may be times that we should keep quiet, avoiding communication as a general rule is sinful. I once read in the newspaper about a couple who were proud of the fact that they had never argued in over 50 years. The husband went on to explain that whenever they disagreed, he would just "keep quiet." Some husbands don't communicate much at all, in order to avoid conflict. We have already discussed why Christians must communicate. We cannot obey God in our marriage without really communicating with our spouse. It is also very easy for bitterness to grow. When there is little or no communication, eventually bitterness will find a way to express itself (Ecclesiastes 3:7b; Ephesians 4:29-31; Colossians 3:19).

- *Stay away from one another*. Obviously this is not an option for Christians. Consider God's commands for wives to respect their husbands, and husbands to love their wives. We are commanded to be "fervent [stretched out with all intensity] in our love" (John 15:12; 1 Peter 4:8).

- *Change the subject*. This tactic is much like the keep-quiet method, but it also involves deception and manipulation (Proverbs 12:22; Proverbs 24:28).

- *Hide information, sins or bitterness*. This method involves deception, which we know to be sin. There is also no way that a couple can be one when this is going on (Genesis 20:2).

Some God-honoring ways to avoid conflict:

- *Seek to know your spouse well, appreciate and understand their perspective* (1 Peter 3:7).

22

- *Gather plenty of data before speaking.* Clarify often what you think you heard or understood. Ask lots of questions (Proverbs 18:13,17).

- Pray, study and think about the issue before speaking, if possible (Proverbs 15:28).

- Demonstrate and/or communicate your love and care at the time of a disagreement (Romans 12:9-10).

- Listen more than you speak, but do speak (Proverbs 10:19; 25:11).

- In matters of sin, approach your spouse in love (Ephesians 4:15; Colossians 3:19).

- In matters of preference, prefer one another (Romans 12:10).

- In matters of wisdom and conscience, suggest searching the Scriptures and getting godly counsel (Proverbs 11:14; 2 Timothy 2:15).

- Refuse to sin in your communication (Proverbs 8:6-8).

- Be more interested in God's glory and the other's good, rather than having your own way, or being right (Joshua 22:5; Romans 15:2).

One of the best ways to avoid conflict when another person is angry at you is to give a gentle and caring answer to their angry words. The Proverbs tell us:

> **A gentle answer turns away wrath, but a harsh word stirs up anger.**
> **Proverbs 15:1**

Be careful that your words are the right words as well. I know of husbands who can say something very unkind or condescending in a calm way to further infuriate their wives. What we are really talking about here is returning good for evil. A humble husband will assume that his wife does have a legitimate point underneath her anger, and he will gently express a desire to hear it. When your wife is upset, you can say something like, "I can see you are upset; let's sit down and talk about it. I do love you and want to work this out."

With a firm commitment, a plan, and a prayer for God "to help in the time of need," we can resist the temptation to return the anger that is coming at us (Hebrews 4:16).

We can usually disarm an angry spouse quite effectively by a godly response. For those rare times when they cannot be disarmed after several tries, the best thing to do is to express your desire to talk when they have calmed down and then walk away. If the situation should ever escalate to physical attack, a couple should seek biblical counseling from their church leadership.

A person who is sincerely and biblically trying to avoid conflict is pursuing peace. Even when there is just one person pursing peace, there will be very little conflict. There may be times when your spouse may not be at peace with you, but you can choose to be at peace with them and seek to reconcile with them.

> **If possible, so far as it depends on you, be at peace with all men.**
> **Romans 12:18**

> **So then let us pursue the things which make for peace and the building up of one another.**
> **Romans 14:19**

Resolving Conflicts

"Okay," you say, "but what about when a conflict has already begun or has been fully carried out (but not resolved), then what?" If you know that your spouse is bitter against you for any reason, you must make every effort to resolve the situation. By not dealing with their bitterness, you risk having anger, and then bitterness takes root in your own heart. There are right and wrong ways to resolve conflicts. Our method of resolving conflicts needs to be in agreement with God's Word.

Some sinful ways to resolve conflicts:

- *Let time heal it.* Healing alone is not what is needed or what honors God when a conflict has taken place. What is needed is confession, forgiveness, and repentance. Time passes for us but not for God. He wants His children to deal with sin quickly (Matthew 5:23-24; Ephesians 4:26). Usually another's sin and our hurts become bigger (not smaller) with the passage of time. Our memories can become very selective and make the resolution process even more difficult.

- *Try to bury it.* Trying to forget about what happened or stay so busy that you don't have time to think only works for so long. A person who lives this way will most likely accumulate many unresolved issues, which can very easily result in more sin, bitterness, depression, and/or even physical sickness. Many misuse Philippians 3:13 in an attempt to biblically justify this position.

- *Pretend it never happened.* This sinful way to resolve conflict is one way to really irritate your spouse! All the pretending in the world does not erase a conflict. A person who does this is not living in reality and will only carry on superficial relationships with other people (Philippians 4:8a).

- *Wait for the other person to initiate the resolution process.* This approach is in direct violation of God's command to go and seek to resolve any problem that someone has with you (Matthew 5:23-24).

- *Punish the other person until they change and take all the blame.* People often do various things to punish their spouse until they change and assume the blame. They may give them the silent treatment, be harsh with them, or even leave. This method of dealing with conflict is only heaping sin upon sin (Galatians 6:1; Romans 12:9-20).

A biblical way to resolve conflict:

- *Confess any sin that you are aware of to God.* Ask Him to open your eyes to any other sin on your part as you consider His Word. You can start by thinking about your motives, your thoughts, your attitude, your words, and your actions (Psalm 139:23-24; 1 John 1:9-10).

- *Go to your spouse, ask forgiveness for each thing you did specifically and discuss your plan not to do those things again* (Ephesians 4:32; James 5:16).

- *Express a desire to resolve the conflict fully and decide together when the best time to do that would be.* Ask if they would (in the meantime) consider if there is any other way that you have sinned, any sin that they may have committed, and what the issues of the conflict are (Proverbs 15:28).

- *Come together at the appointed time.* Express your desire to honor God and love one another by doing everything you can to resolve this issue with both of you on the same team against the problem, not against each other (Psalm 34:14). Think of the problem as not between you but as a challenge for both of you together.

- *Pray together for God's wisdom, self-control, and speech* (Proverbs 16:32; James 1:5).

- *Review God's rules of communication.* Decide on a reminder phrase or sign you can use if there is a violation during your discussion (Ephesians 4:15, 26-32; James 1:19).

  1. Be a good listener
  2. Speak the truth.
  3. Speak in a righteous way—in love.
  4. Speak with the right purposes: God's glory and the other's good.
  5. Speak as clearly as possible.

- *Each one should take a turn to confess any sin that has not been confessed (to God and spouse), and ask forgiveness.* Each should ask for the other's input (Ephesians 4:32; James 5:16; 1 John 1:9).

- *Begin discussing the issues that precipitated the conflict.* Let me suggest maybe spending only 30-40 minutes trying to reach a point of unity concerning the issue (at least come up with a plan). After that, decide on another time to come together again. Seek to love one another in the meantime.

- Decide what you can agree upon (each takes a turn).
- Decide what you do not agree upon (each takes a turn).
- Decide what kind of issue(s) you are dealing with (each offers input).

  Is it a preference issue? Discuss ways to prefer one another (Philippians 2:3-5).

  Is it a sin issue? Discuss a repentance plan (Ephesians 4:22-24).

  Is it a conscience issue? Study and get counsel but do not ask the other to go against their conscience until the thing in question can be done in faith (Romans 14:23).

  Is it a wisdom issue? Gather facts, study, get counsel, and have each spouse give input. Then you are to make a biblical leadership decision as the husband. At this point the wife should submit and trust in God's sovereignty, unless the husband is asking her to sin (Proverbs 2:3-6; Proverbs 12:15; 2 Timothy 2:15).

- Decide on specific steps to resolve the issue (each offers input).
- Together begin carrying out the appropriate steps to resolve the issue.
- Decide if and when you need to discuss the issue again.
- End your time together with prayer and an expression of love.

This resolution process encourages both husband and wife to remain humble, self-controlled, and solution-oriented. It is especially good for couples who are just starting to resolve issues biblically. Though it may take more than one time, it should help to resolve any issue. If you as a couple should be unsuccessful in reaching a point of unity after three tries, the wisest thing to do is enlist another godly couple to assist you. They should be able to determine what is keeping you from resolving the issue.

Avoiding conflict and resolving conflict will take repeated practice for those who have already created bad habits in this area. The good news is, if you persevere through the learning process, you will begin to enjoy the fruit of your labor. Handling personal differences, differences of opinion, and conflict God's way will cause love and unity to grow in your marriage, and both of you to grow in wisdom.

Who among you is wise and understanding? Let him show by his good behavior his deeds in the gentleness of wisdom. But if you have bitter jealousy and selfish ambition in your heart, do not be arrogant and so lie against the truth. This wisdom is not that which comes down from above, but is earthly, natural, demonic. For where jealousy and selfish ambition exist, there is disorder and every evil thing. But the wisdom from above is first pure, then peaceable, gentle, reasonable, full of mercy and good fruits, unwavering, without hypocrisy. And the seed whose fruit is righteousness is sown in peace by those who make peace.

James 3:13-18

GOD'S PROVISIONS FOR MAN

God specifically provided for our needs. He has made a way for our salvation, our sanctification, and our glorification. If you partake of these three provisions you can become the man you were created to be.

1.   God's provision of salvation

God has provided a Savior in the person of Jesus Christ. Amazingly, He was willing to pay the penalty for the sin that *we* owe. This means that even though Jesus lived a sinless life, He, Almighty God, left heaven and the adoration He deserves in order to endure the conditions of this world, suffer shame, be rejected by men, die a criminal's gruesome death, bear the guilt of all our sins, be bitterly rejected by the Father (with whom He knew only love and harmony), and suffer the hell we so richly deserve (Philippians 2:6-8). Only Christ could do what was necessary to bring us to God.

> **For Christ also died for sins once for all, the just for the unjust, so that He might** *bring us to God*, **having been put to death in the flesh, but made alive in the spirit.**
> **1 Peter 3:18 [emphasis mine]**

It was through Christ's suffering and rejection on the cross that God's righteous wrath against sin was satisfied and a way to obtain forgiveness was made (Romans 5:9). This forgiveness is possible because God is willing to exchange Christ's righteousness for our sinfulness (2 Corinthians 5:21). For this exchange to take place a husband must have saving faith. Saving faith involves:

- Acknowledging the true reason for our existence and God's full right to our lives and how we live them (Matthew 16:24-26; Romans 11:36; 1 Corinthians 6:20).
- Coming to God in humbleness, recognizing you have nothing to offer God in your defense (James 4:6).
- Asking Him for His mercy and forgiveness, instead of what is deserved (Luke 18:9-14).

- Believing in who Christ is and His payment for your sin (1 Corinthians 15:3).
- Believing that Christ rose from the dead as Lord over all and sits at the right hand of the Father pleading the case of all those who believe (1 Corinthians 15:4; Philippians 2:9-11; Hebrews 7:25).

Christ also taught that in order to enter the kingdom of God we must be like a little child. This may smack at our manly pride but Christ was talking about important attitudes of the heart. A little child knows his place and has humble faith. A little child is dependent and needy. We must come to God with this kind of faith in order to receive His gift of salvation.

> **"Truly I say to you, whoever does not receive the kingdom of God like a child will by no means enter it at all."**
> **Mark 10:15**

If we really contemplate saving faith, we can understand why Christ said what He did to those who came to hear Him speak.

> **"Enter through the narrow gate; for the gate is wide and the way is broad that leads to destruction, and there are many who enter through it. For the gate is small and the way is narrow that leads to life, and** *there are few who find it.***"**
> **Matthew 7:13-14 [emphasis mine]**

Don't be deceived. A prayer said or a profession made in the past should not assure you of your salvation. Are you *having* saving faith *now*? Are you believing *now*? It is an ongoing (obedient and persevering) belief that demonstrates that you are a child of God. Christ offered this warning to all who would listen,

> **"Not everyone who says to Me, 'Lord, Lord,' will enter the kingdom of heaven."**
> **Matthew 7:21a**

If you have never yielded to God's plan (to be forgiven and walk with Him) I beseech you, take time right now to talk to Him about these things. Ask Him to be merciful to you, not because you deserve it, but because you know that He is the Lord God who created the universe. Confess your sins (of motive, thought, word and deed) to God and seek His forgiveness on the basis of Christ's payment for your sin. If you come to God in humility and with saving faith, He will grant you salvation.

> **[Jesus said] "All that the Father gives Me will come to Me, and the one who comes to Me I will certainly not cast out."**
> **John 6:37**

2. God's provision of sanctification

Salvation does not automatically cause us to be all that we should be. Not by a long shot! It does, however, mean that we will wholeheartedly enter into a dependent effort with God toward *change* into Christlikeness (Philippians 3:12-14; 2 Peter 3:18). We do this moment by moment because of and by the Power of the gospel. In our daily lives we must remember and apply the gospel truths. (Christ's life, Christ's death for our sin, Christ in us, Christ for us, etc.)

Sometimes we may be inclined to believe that little can be done to change our ways, but obviously this is wrong. Once we are saved, God initiates the sanctification or *growth process*. God Himself provides His Word, His Spirit, prayer, and His Church for our growth (2 Peter 1:2-11). Without these provisions we could not change in the least. On the other hand, God commands that we "exercise ourselves unto godliness" (1Timothy 4:7-9). What does this mean? The Greek word for "exercise" (*gumnazo*) is where our words gymnasium and gymnastics come from. This means that with prayer for God's help we are to put a strenuous effort into becoming more like Christ. When we do our part, we must also trust in God's work and God's promise, on the basis of what Christ did on the cross for us.

> **For I am confident of this very thing, that He who began a good work in you will perfect it until the day of Christ Jesus.**
> **Philippians 1:6**

When we do our part as a Christian, we are cooperating with God in the growth process. We do our part, first of all, by *devoting our lives to loving and living for Him, <u>rather than self</u>*. When a person truly comes to faith in Christ he will have a new passion—Christ.

And He died for all, so that they who live should no longer live for themselves, but for Him who died and rose again on their behalf.
2 Corinthians 5:15

We are to be so devoted to our Creator, that we labor to please Him with every fiber of our being. Our love for the God who created and saved us should be so great that walking with Him is more important to us than anything else in the world.

Dependently working with God in the change process also means that *we will deal with any known sin <u>God's way</u>*. Some people believe that God's way of dealing with sin is to simply confess it and ask forgiveness. The Bible teaches that we are to deal with our sin in a fuller and much more practical way.

When we sin, God wants us to do three things:

- Confess to God our sin and our resolve to change toward righteousness. (Proverbs 28:13; 1 John 1:9)
- Rejoice in forgiveness through Christ (Matthew 6:12).
- Ask God for His transforming grace to change. (Psalm 25:4; John 15:5).
- Repent according to God's process for change by:
  a. *Working to renew the mind with Scripture* . (Romans 12:1-2). This involves knowing Scripture about whatever sin issue is at hand well enough to *specifically* change wrong or incomplete thinking into thinking that is in agreement with God's principles and promises. We must purposefully guard and renew our minds.
  b. *Working to put off sinful actions and to put on righteous ones* (Ephesians 4:20-24). This involves putting enough thought into one's life to: (1) specifically plan how and when a particular sin will be avoided, and (2) determine specific ways to apply its righteous alternatives. True repentance does not take place without these things.

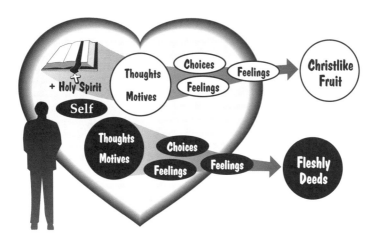

We must renew our minds because our actions flow out of our motives, thoughts and beliefs. This fact can be pictured something like this.

3.   God's provision of glorification

God promises to bring us to heaven where He is and to free us from our sinful bent (1 Corinthians 15:50-58). What a great hope we have! This life is not all there is! Our short time on Earth is not what life is even about. Everything is working toward the great end of God's people being with Him for eternity (Revelation 21:3, 7).

Every Christian needs to be heavenly-minded (Colossians 3:1-3; Matthew 6:33). We will look forward to heaven more if we fully accept the fact that this life is *not* heaven, and never will be. If we live with heaven in our sights we will please God and be less likely to grow weary in the hardships of life (Hebrews 11:8-10; 12:1-3). Remembering that we will see Jesus face to face one day can also have a very purifying affect on our lives (1 John 3:2-3). We should strive to keep an eternal perspective and place *all* our hope in our future with Christ.

> **Therefore, prepare your minds for action, keep sober in spirit, fix your hope completely on the grace to be brought to you at the revelation of Jesus Christ.**
>
> **1 Peter 1:13**

Replacing Sinful Habits	
Sinful Thoughts, Void of God	**Thankful, Trusting, Hopeful Thoughts**
I've had it! I can't take this job anymore. (discouragement / giving up)	Lord, You know all about this difficult situation. Thank you that I have a job and that you can help me to endure. I pray that you might supply a different job if that is best. (Philippians 2:14; 4:13)
I just want to be left alone. (selfishness)	Lord, You know I don't feel like giving right now but I thank you that I have a family and that you can give me your strength. Help me to serve you and others now. (Philippians 2:3-4)
What if I lose my job? (worry)	Lord, I pray that I don't lose my job but if I do, I know that you will somehow provide. I thank you that you are faithful and in control. I trust you. (Matthew 6:25-34)

Communication and Conflict Resolution is excerpted from the book, **The Exemplary Husband: A Biblical Perspective** by Dr. Stuart Scott. Available to go along with this book are the study guide and teacher's guide.

From Pride to Humility and **Anger, Anxiety and Fear** are two other booklets excerpted from **The Exemplary Husband: A Biblical Perspective.**

Other titles by Stuart Scott:
Killing Sin Habits
Biblical Manhood

Find these and other titles at **www.focuspublishing.com** or call Focus Publishing at 1-800-913-6287.

Quantity discounts available by phone.

Focus Publishing, Inc.
Bemidji, MN